In a world of wonder, both young and old,

Where lessons of life are worth their weight in gold,

From responsibility's call to honesty's grace,

These teachings guide us through life's complex maze.

With kindness as our compass, we find our way,

Sharing, and gratitude, bring light to our day.

Patience and courage, we must not neglect,

Respect for differences, we must protect.

Empathy's bridge connects hearts near and far,

Perseverance shines like the brightest star.

Respecting nature, together we stand,

In teamwork, we thrive, hand in hand.

Kindness as our gift, sharing our creed,

In a world of gratitude, our souls find what they need.

The courage to be honest, a treasure to behold,

As we gather the stories that time has told....**cont'd**

Listening with care, we truly understand,

The joy of learning, it's all in our hand.

Respecting our elders, their wisdom we glean,

Imagination's key, a world we can dream.

Generosity's magic, it's a gift that we share,

In forgiveness and patience, we learn how to care.

Through the power of empathy, we bridge each divide,

With imagination, our hearts open wide.

The beauty of friendships, like flowers in bloom,

In positivity's realm, we chase away gloom.

The strength of perseverance, a force hard to beat,

In the beauty of nature, our lives feel complete.

As curiosity leads us through journeys unknown,

In empathy's embrace, we're never alone.

In knowledge, we find treasures in every nook,

And, in honesty, we write our life's book....**cont'd**

With each lesson's guidance, we learn to be strong,

In kindness and empathy, we all truly belong.

In the world we create, let these lessons shine bright,

Guiding us through life, from morning to night.

For in following these lessons, we shape our own fate,

In the story of life, let's make each day great.

With hearts full of love, together we strive,

To make this world better, as long as we're alive.

Table of Contents

Lesson 1: Kindness

Lesson 2: Sharing

Lesson 3: Gratitude

Lesson 4: Patience

Lesson 5: Courage

Lesson 6: Respect for Differences

Lesson 7: Empathy

Lesson 8: Perseverance Pays Off

Lesson 9: Respect for Nature

Lesson 10: Teamwork Triumphs

Lesson 11: Respect for Others

Lesson 12: The Gift of Kindness

Lesson 13: Honesty and Trust

Lesson 14: The Magic of Sharing Knowledge

Lesson 15: The Power of Forgiveness

Lesson 16: The Magic of Curiosity

Lesson 17: The Beauty of Friendship Bonds

Lesson 18: The Gift of Positivity

Lesson 19: The Strength of Empathy

Lesson 20: The Magic of Imagination

Lesson 21: The Gift of Respect for Elders

Lesson 22: The Art of Patience

Lesson 23: The Gift of Generosity

Lesson 24: The Magic of Perseverance

Lesson 25: The Gift of Listening

Lesson 26: The Joy of Learning

Lesson 27: Gratitude for Family

Lesson 28: The Adventure of Honesty

Lesson 29: Sharing Makes Friends

Lesson 30: Listen Carefully

Lesson 31: Be Grateful

Lesson 32: The Joy of Giving

Lesson 33: The Magic of Teamwork

Lesson 34: The Power of Adaptability

Lesson 35: The Treasure of Time

Lesson 36: The Wonders of Exploration

Lesson 37: The Magic of Dreams

Lesson 38: The Art of Communication

Lesson 39: The Importance of Laughter

Lesson 40: The Gift of Giving Back

Lesson 41: The Joy of Trying New Things

Lesson 42: The Magic of Music

Lesson 43: The Power of Empowerment

Lesson 44: The Treasure of Good Manners

Lesson 45: The Strength of Self-Belief

Lesson 46: The Gift of Resourcefulness

Lesson 47: The Joy of Helping Others

Lesson 48: The Magic of Problem Solving

Lesson 1: Kindness Matters

Understanding: Being kind means treating others with respect and empathy.

Real Life Application: Help a friend in need, share your toys, and be polite to others.

Story: The Adventures of Kip the Kangaroo

In the enchanting Outback, lived Kip the Kangaroo, known for his boundless kindness. One hot summer day, Kip found a thirsty bird named Bella who had lost her way. He hopped to the nearest waterhole and offered Bella a cool drink from his pouch. Grateful for Kip's kindness, Bella sang a beautiful song that echoed through the Outback, bringing new friends to join their picnic by the water.

As Kip and Bella's kindness spread, they embarked on an adventure through the Outback. They met a wise old koala named Ollie, who shared stories of how kindness had helped the animals of the Outback survive and thrive. Kip, Bella, and Ollie decided to host a Kindness Carnival for all the animals, filled with games, laughter, and acts of kindness.

Kip and Bella's kindness not only strengthened their friendship but also created a ripple effect of good deeds throughout the Outback, reminding everyone that kindness was the most magical treasure of all.

Consequence of Not Using: If you're unkind, people may not want to be around you, and you might feel lonely.

Questions for Children:

1. Can you name three ways to show kindness to others?

2. How does it make you feel when someone is kind to you?

Perhaps you could write something here about this lesson' maybe your own experiences or how you could use it yourself, maybe make a promise.

I promise never to be unkind and to just be my kind + caring self

Lesson 2: Honesty is the Best Policy

Understanding: Honesty means telling the truth, even when it's difficult.

Real Life Application: Always tell the truth, even if you've made a mistake.

Story: The Quest of Prince Leo and the Magic Mirror

In the kingdom of Verityville, there was a magic mirror that only revealed the truth. Prince Leo discovered it while exploring his father's castle. He asked the mirror if he was the best archer in the land, but the mirror showed his true skills. Leo knew he needed to practice harder, so he committed himself to becoming the best archer through honesty and dedication.

As Leo's archery skills improved, he met other young knights who admired his hard work and dedication. They started the "Honest Knights" club, where they not only honed their skills but also helped others in the kingdom. They organized archery competitions and awarded prizes to those who displayed honesty and integrity.

Their club flourished, and Prince Leo became known not only for his archery but also for his unwavering honesty. He grew up to be a beloved and respected ruler who valued truth and fairness above all.

Consequence of Not Using: If you're not honest, people may not trust you.

Questions for Children:

1. Can you think of a time when telling the truth was hard but important?

2. How do you feel when someone lies to you?

Perhaps you could write something here about this lesson' maybe your own experiences or how you could use it yourself, maybe make a promise.

> I promise to always tell the truth even if I get into trubble and if you lie you'll be in even more trubble.
> † ✵

Lesson 3: Sharing Makes Friends

Understanding: Sharing means giving part of what you have to someone else.

Real Life Application: Share your toys, snacks, or time with a friend.

Story: The Tale of Luna and the Magic Seeds

In the secret Garden of Serendipity, Luna the fox discovered magical seeds that grew into beautiful flowers. She decided to share these seeds with her animal friends. Luna's act of generosity not only brought her friends together but also attracted butterflies, bees, and birds who helped her garden bloom into the most splendid place in the forest. It became a haven for all creatures to enjoy together.

The creatures of the garden decided to organize a grand celebration. They created fun games like hide-and-seek among the flowers, flying races with the butterflies, and a special feast with fruits from the garden. New friendships bloomed, and Luna's garden became a place of joy and togetherness for all.

Consequence of Not Using: If you don't share, you might not have as many friends to play with.

Questions for Children:

1. How does sharing make you feel?

2. Why is it important to share with others?

Perhaps you could write something here about this lesson' maybe your own experiences or how you could use it yourself, maybe make a promise.

Lesson 4: Listen Carefully

Understanding: Listening carefully means paying attention when others are speaking.

Real Life Application: When someone is talking to you, look at them and don't interrupt.

Story: The Tale of Sammy the Squirrel's Adventure

In the Whispering Woods, Sammy the squirrel set out on a grand adventure. His friends gave him important advice before he left. They told him to listen carefully to the rustling leaves, the bubbling brooks, and the wise old owls.

As Sammy journeyed through the Whispering Woods, he encountered many challenges. The rustling leaves whispered secrets that led him to hidden treasures, and the bubbling brooks shared stories of the forest's history. Sammy listened closely and learned about the lives of the creatures around him, forging new friendships.

One day, he met the wise old owl, Olivia, who shared the forest's deepest mysteries. Thanks to Sammy's attentive ears, he returned home with tales of his thrilling adventure and a deeper understanding of the Whispering Woods.

Consequence of Not Using: If you don't listen, you might miss important information or upset others.

Questions for Children:

1. Why is it important to listen when others are talking?
2. How does it feel when someone doesn't listen to you?

Perhaps you could write something here about this lesson' maybe your own experiences or how you could use it yourself, maybe make a promise.

I promise that if I am talking I'll look at the person who's is the teacher and same with listning. *

Lesson 5: Be Grateful

Understanding: Gratitude means being thankful for the things you have.

Real Life Application: Say "thank you" when someone is kind to you, and appreciate your family and friends.

Story: The Tale of Ellie's Grateful Garden

In the village of Thanksburg, Ellie had a magical garden. It blossomed with the most vibrant flowers and delicious fruits. Every morning, she thanked the sun, the rain, and the soil for their gifts.

One day, a young traveler visited the village. Ellie shared her bountiful harvest with the traveler, and they enjoyed a feast together. The traveler, impressed by Ellie's kindness and gratitude, gifted her a rare seed. When planted, it grew into a tree that bore enchanted fruits, spreading happiness and thankfulness throughout the land.

Consequence of Not Using: If you're not grateful, people may not want to help or give to you.

Questions for Children:

1. What are you thankful for in your life?

2. How does saying "thank you" make you feel?

Perhaps you could write something here about this lesson' maybe your own experiences or how you could use it yourself, maybe make a promise.

Lesson 6: Responsibility Matters

Understanding: Responsibility means taking care of your tasks and doing your part.

Real Life Application: Complete your homework, chores, and take care of your pets.

Story: The Adventures of Ruby the Responsible Rabbit

In the peaceful village of Dutiful Dale, Ruby the Rabbit was known for her sense of responsibility. One day, a storm threatened the village. While some animals were nervous, Ruby sprang into action. She helped her neighbors secure their homes, collect food, and find shelter.

As the storm raged on, the animals of Dutiful Dale realized they had to work together. Ruby took charge, organizing teams to mend the damaged houses and provide food for those in need. Her actions united the village, and they weathered the storm with courage and unity.

Consequence of Not Using: If you're not responsible, important tasks may be left undone, causing problems for you and others.

Questions for Children:

1. What are some tasks you are responsible for at home or school?

2. How does it feel when someone is not responsible?

Perhaps you could write something here about this lesson' maybe your own experiences or how you could use it yourself, maybe make a promise.

Lesson 7: Empathy and Understanding

Understanding: Empathy means understanding how others feel and showing kindness towards them.

Real Life Application: Be a good listener, help a friend who's sad, and be there for others when they need support.

Story: The Tale of Emma the Empathetic Elephant

In the heart of the Enchanted Savannah, Emma the Elephant possessed a remarkable gift — empathy. She could sense the feelings of other animals in the Savannah, and she used her gift to offer comfort and support to those in need.

One day, Emma noticed a lonely lion named Leo, who had lost his way. She approached him with gentle words and a listening ear. Leo shared his worries and fears with Emma, who empathized with his feelings and helped him find his way back to his family.

As Emma's reputation for empathy spread, the animals of the Savannah started coming to her with their concerns. She organized group activities and shared stories that encouraged understanding and kindness. The Savannah became a place where every animal felt heard and valued.

Consequence of Not Using: If you lack empathy, you may not be able to support others effectively, and they may feel isolated.

Questions for Children:

1. How can you show empathy towards a friend who is sad or upset?

2. Why is it important to understand how others feel?

Perhaps you could write something here about this lesson' maybe your own experiences or how you could use it yourself, maybe make a promise.

Lesson 8: Perseverance Pays Off

Understanding: Perseverance means not giving up, even when things are difficult.

Real Life Application: Keep trying when you face challenges, practice to improve your skills, and work hard to achieve your goals.

Story: The Quest of Timmy the Tortoise

In the Land of Patience, lived Timmy the Tortoise, known for his remarkable perseverance. One sunny day, he heard about a great race that was taking place in the neighboring kingdom. Many animals were competing, including speedy hares and agile cheetahs.

Timmy decided to participate, even though he was the slowest of all. While others mocked him, he practiced every day, taking slow and steady steps. The race began, and Timmy lagged behind, but he never gave up.

As the other animals grew tired, Timmy, with his unwavering determination, overtook them one by one. In the end, he won the race through his patience and perseverance. The kingdom celebrated his triumph, and the other animals learned the value of persistence.

Consequence of Not Using: If you give up easily, you may miss out on opportunities and the chance to improve.

Questions for Children:

1. Can you think of a time when you had to work hard and persevere to achieve something?

2. Why is it important to never give up?

Perhaps you could write something here about this lesson' maybe your own experiences or how you could use it yourself, maybe make a promise.

Lesson 9: Respect for Nature

Understanding: Respect for nature means caring for the environment and the creatures that share the planet with us.

Real Life Application: Pick up litter, conserve water and energy, and treat animals with kindness.

Story: The Quest of Maya the Nature Guardian

In the mystical Forest of Harmony, Maya, a young guardian, was chosen by the ancient spirits to protect the forest and its creatures. She felt a deep connection with the animals and the trees and understood the importance of respecting nature.

One day, she discovered that the magical river, the life force of the forest, was polluted by careless travelers. Maya embarked on a journey to educate people about the importance of respecting the environment. She organized cleanup days and planted new trees. Her dedication to the forest inspired the travelers to change their ways.

The once-polluted river became crystal clear, and the animals of the forest thrived. Maya's respect for nature had a profound impact, and her forest remained a haven for generations to come.

Consequence of Not Using: If we don't respect nature, we harm our planet, leading to pollution, deforestation, and harm to wildlife.

Questions for Children:

1. What are some ways you can show respect for nature and the environment?

2. Why is it important to protect the environment?

Perhaps you could write something here about this lesson' maybe your own experiences or how you could use it yourself, maybe make a promise.

Lesson 10: Teamwork Triumphs

Understanding: Teamwork means working together with others to achieve a common goal.

Real Life Application: Cooperate with your classmates on group projects, play team sports, and help your family with chores.

Story: The Quest of the Diverse Crew

In the Kingdom of Unity, there was a legendary spaceship known as "Harmony Star." It could only be piloted by a diverse crew of animals with unique talents. A rabbit named Roger was an expert navigator, a squirrel named Sandy had quick reflexes, and a parrot named Polly was a skilled communicator.

One day, a meteor shower threatened their kingdom, and they were called into action. With teamwork and coordination, they guided the spaceship through the meteor shower, ensuring the safety of the kingdom. Each crew member's skills were essential, and they knew that by working together, they could achieve great things.

Their adventure inspired other animals to embrace teamwork and appreciate the power of diversity.

Consequence of Not Using: Without teamwork, it's challenging to accomplish larger goals and solve complex problems.

Questions for Children:

1. Can you think of a time when you worked as part of a team? How did it feel?

2. Why is teamwork important in our daily lives?

Perhaps you could write something here about this lesson' maybe your own experiences or how you could use it yourself, maybe make a promise.

Lesson 11: Patience in Practice

Understanding: Patience means waiting calmly for something without getting upset or frustrated.

Real Life Application: Be patient while waiting in line, for your turn, or for things to happen.

Story: The Quest of Pippin the Penguin

In the frosty lands of Chillington, Pippin the Penguin was known for his remarkable patience. One winter, he set off on a journey to find the mythical Ice Crystal, a rare gem said to bring endless happiness. His journey was fraught with challenges, from treacherous icy winds to slippery slopes.

With each obstacle, Pippin exercised his patience, taking slow, steady steps and learning to appreciate the beauty of the icy world around him. Finally, he found the Ice Crystal at the heart of the frozen glacier, and it shone with a gentle, soothing light. Pippin's patience had led him to the greatest treasure of all.

Consequence of Not Using: If you're impatient, you may become stressed and miss out on the beauty of the journey.

Questions for Children:

1. Can you think of a time when you needed to be patient?

2. Why is patience important in our daily lives?

Perhaps you could write something here about this lesson' maybe your own experiences or how you could use it yourself, maybe make a promise.

Lesson 12: The Power of Imagination

Understanding: Imagination means creating stories, ideas, and pictures in your mind.

Real Life Application: Use your imagination to solve problems, create art, and have fun adventures.

Story: The Tale of Lily's Magical Sketchbook

In the town of Wonderwood, Lily was a young artist with an extraordinary imagination. She had a magical sketchbook that turned her drawings into real adventures. One day, she drew a sailing ship on the open sea, and the next moment, she was aboard with her animal friends.

As they sailed to distant lands, they encountered friendly sea creatures and explored hidden islands. Lily's imagination led to thrilling quests, new friends, and unforgettable experiences. She learned that the power of imagination could create extraordinary journeys right at her fingertips.

Consequence of Not Using: Without imagination, life may seem less exciting and creative.

Questions for Children:

1. How can you use your imagination to make your day more fun?

2. Why is imagination important in problem-solving?

Perhaps you could write something here about this lesson' maybe your own experiences or how you could use it yourself, maybe make a promise.

So I have a big imagination and I pretended to fight wolves and a mate was absolutely scared out of his skin and had nightmayers.

Lesson 13: Generosity of Spirit

Understanding: Generosity of spirit means giving from the heart without expecting anything in return.

Real Life Application: Be generous with compliments, help those in need, and share your time and resources.

Story: The Tale of Marco and the Magic Pebble

In the charming village of Heartstone, there was a legend about the Magic Pebble. It was said that anyone who gave without expecting something in return would be granted a wish. Marco, a young boy, took this to heart and decided to test the legend.

One day, he found an old woman struggling to carry groceries. Marco offered his help, and the woman's eyes twinkled with gratitude. She gave him a simple pebble and said, "You have a generous spirit." Later, when Marco wished for happiness, the pebble's magic made his heart glow with joy. He had discovered that true happiness came from giving selflessly.

Consequence of Not Using: If you're not generous, you might miss out on the happiness that comes from helping others.

Questions for Children:

1. Can you think of a time when you were generous to someone?

2. How does it feel to receive a generous act of kindness?

> Perhaps you could write something here about this lesson' maybe your own experiences or how you could use it yourself, maybe make a promise.

Lesson 14: Adaptability and Change

Understanding: Adaptability means being able to change or adjust to new situations or circumstances.

Real Life Application: Embrace change with an open mind, learn from new experiences, and stay flexible.

Story: The Quest of Mia the Chameleon*

In the vibrant Rainforest of Evergreen, Mia the Chameleon was known for her adaptability. She could change her colors and adapt to any environment. One day, the rainforest faced a long, harsh drought. Many creatures struggled to find water and food.

Mia used her adaptability to help her friends. She climbed to the highest tree and changed her colors to signal the location of waterholes and food sources. Her quick thinking and adaptability saved the rainforest's inhabitants from hardship.

Consequence of Not Using: If you're not adaptable, you might find it challenging to cope with change and unexpected situations.

Questions for Children:

1. How can you adapt to new situations or changes in your life?

2. Why is adaptability an important skill to have?

Perhaps you could write something here about this lesson' maybe your own experiences or how you could use it yourself, maybe make a promise.

Lesson 15: Courage in the Face of Fear

Understanding: Courage means facing something scary or difficult with bravery and determination.

Real Life Application: Stand up to bullies, try new things, and face your fears with confidence.

Story: The Adventures of Leo the Lionheart*

In the Kingdom of Valiance, Leo the Lion was known for his bravery. One day, a fierce dragon terrorized the kingdom, breathing fire and causing destruction. Most of the animals fled in fear, but Leo stood his ground.

He decided to confront the dragon to protect his home. With unwavering courage, he approached the dragon and engaged it in a conversation. He discovered that the dragon was lonely and frightened itself. Leo's compassion and bravery helped the dragon find a new home, and peace was restored to the kingdom.

Consequence of Not Using: If you lack courage, you might miss out on opportunities and let fear control your actions.

Questions for Children:

1. Can you think of a time when you were brave in the face of fear?

2. Why is courage important in life?

Perhaps you could write something here about this lesson' maybe your own experiences or how you could use it yourself, maybe make a promise.

Lesson 16: Honoring Differences

Understanding: Honoring differences means respecting and valuing people who are unique in their own way.

Real Life Application: Celebrate diversity, make friends from different backgrounds, and avoid making fun of others.

*Story: The Tale of Maya and the Magical Mosaic**

In the village of Multiville, Maya discovered a hidden cave filled with magical mosaic tiles. Each tile represented a different culture and background. She decided to create a mosaic that celebrated the diversity of her village.

Maya's project brought the community together. People from all backgrounds shared stories, songs, and dances. The mosaic became a symbol of unity and a reminder to honor the differences that made their village vibrant and beautiful.

Consequence of Not Using: If you don't honor differences, you may miss out on learning about other cultures and making wonderful friends.

Questions for Children:

1. How can you show respect for people from different backgrounds?

2. Why is it important to celebrate diversity?

Perhaps you could write something here about this lesson' maybe your own experiences or how you could use it yourself, maybe make a promise.

Lesson 17: Responsibility in Actions

Understanding: Responsibility in actions means being accountable for your behavior and choices.

Real Life Application: Apologize when you make a mistake, own up to your actions, and take care of your belongings.

*Story: The Adventures of Benny the Bear**

In the Bearington Woods, Benny the Bear was known for his sense of responsibility. One day, a storm hit the woods, and Benny noticed that a tree he had been climbing was damaged by lightning. He knew he had been too rough on it and decided to take responsibility.

Benny organized a group of animal friends to repair the tree. They worked together, making the woods safer for all. Benny learned that taking responsibility for his actions not only improved his surroundings but also earned the respect of his friends.

Consequence of Not Using: If you're not responsible in your actions, you might damage things and harm relationships.

Questions for Children:

1. Can you think of a time when you took responsibility for something you did?
2. How does it feel when someone apologizes for their actions?

Perhaps you could write something here about this lesson' maybe your own experiences or how you could use it yourself, maybe make a promise.

Lesson 18: Friendship and Loyalty

Understanding: Friendship and loyalty mean being a good friend, staying true to your friends, and supporting them.

Real Life Application: Be there for your friends when they need you, stand up for them, and make time for your friends.

*Story: The Tale of Finn and the Golden Thread**

In the Kingdom of Harmony, there was a legend about a magical Golden Thread. Whoever possessed it had the power to bind the strongest friendships. Finn, a young fox, found a part of the Golden Thread while exploring the forest.

He realized the value of friendship and decided to share it with his friends. Each friend received a piece of the Golden Thread, and they made a pact to always be there for each other. Their loyalty and friendship were unbreakable, and they faced every challenge as a team.

Consequence of Not Using: If you're not a good friend or loyal, you may lose valuable friendships.

Questions for Children:

1. What qualities make a good friend?
2. Why is loyalty important in a friendship?

> Perhaps you could write something here about this lesson' maybe your own experiences or how you could use it yourself, maybe make a promise.
>
> I used to have a freind called Lewis and 20th NOV 2023 He said "Hey Cody your a rubish keeper and never make it pro. shshshshsh. HA HA HA!!

Lesson 19: The Joy of Learning

Understanding: The joy of learning means finding happiness in discovering new things and gaining knowledge.

Real Life Application: Be curious, ask questions, read books, and explore new subjects.

*Story: The Quest of Oliver and the Book of Wonders**

In the Library of Enchantment, Oliver, a young owl, found an ancient Book of Wonders. The book contained stories of faraway lands, magical creatures, and hidden secrets. Oliver was fascinated and decided to embark on a quest to uncover these wonders.

As he read and learned, he shared the stories with his friends, and they all became curious about the world around them. Together, they discovered that the joy of learning was a magical journey in itself, full of surprises and endless possibilities.

Consequence of Not Using: If you don't embrace the joy of learning, you may miss out on the excitement of discovering new things.

Questions for Children:

1. What do you enjoy learning about the most?

2. Why is learning important in life?

Perhaps you could write something here about this lesson' maybe your own experiences or how you could use it yourself, maybe make a promise.

I ♥ ♥ ♥
LEARNING
I ♥ ✳ 📖

Lesson 20: Gratitude for Family

Understanding: Gratitude for family means being thankful for the love and support of your family members.

Real Life Application: Say "thank you" to your family, spend quality time together, and express your love for them.

Story: The Tale of Mia's Magical Thank-You Letters

Mia was a young mouse who discovered the magic of thank-you letters. She wrote heartfelt notes to her family, thanking them for their love and support. Her letters brought smiles and warmth to her family's hearts.

In return, Mia's family organized a special day to express their gratitude. They spent the day together, sharing stories, playing games, and enjoying a picnic. Their love and appreciation for one another made their family bonds even stronger.

Consequence of Not Using: If you don't show gratitude for your family, you might take them for granted and miss opportunities for meaningful connections.

Questions for Children:

1. Why is it important to be grateful for your family?
2. How can you express your gratitude to your family members?

Perhaps you could write something here about this lesson' maybe your own experiences or how you could use it yourself, maybe make a promise.

Lesson 21: Honesty is the Best Policy

Understanding: Honesty means telling the truth, even when it's difficult.

Real Life Application: Always tell the truth, even if you've made a mistake.

Story: The Quest of Prince Leo and the Magic Mirror

In the kingdom of Verityville, there was a magic mirror that only revealed the truth. Prince Leo discovered it while exploring his father's castle. He asked the mirror if he was the best archer in the land, but the mirror showed his true skills. Leo knew he needed to practice harder, so he committed himself to becoming the best archer through honesty and dedication.

As Leo's archery skills improved, he met other young knights who admired his hard work and dedication. They started the "Honest Knights" club, where they not only honed their skills but also helped others in the kingdom. They organized archery competitions and awarded prizes to those who displayed honesty and integrity.

Their club flourished, and Prince Leo became known not only for his archery but also for his unwavering honesty. He grew up to be a beloved and respected ruler who valued truth and fairness above all.

Consequence of Not Using: If you're not honest, people may not trust you.

Questions for Children:

1. Can you think of a time when telling the truth was hard but important?

2. How do you feel when someone lies to you?

Perhaps you could write something here about this lesson' maybe your own experiences or how you could use it yourself, maybe make a promise.

Lesson 22: Sharing Makes Friends

Understanding: Sharing means giving part of what you have to someone else.

Real Life Application: Share your toys, snacks, or time with a friend.

Story: The Tale of Luna and the Magic Seeds

In the secret Garden of Serendipity, Luna the fox discovered magical seeds that grew into beautiful flowers. She decided to share these seeds with her animal friends. Luna's act of generosity not only brought her friends together but also attracted butterflies, bees, and birds who helped her garden bloom into the most splendid place in the forest. It became a haven for all creatures to enjoy together.

The creatures of the garden decided to organize a grand celebration. They created fun games like hide-and-seek among the flowers, flying races with the butterflies, and a special feast with fruits from the garden. New friendships bloomed, and Luna's garden became a place of joy and togetherness for all.

Consequence of Not Using: If you don't share, you might not have as many friends to play with.

Questions for Children:

1. How does sharing make you feel?
2. Why is it important to share with others?

Perhaps you could write something here about this lesson' maybe your own experiences or how you could use it yourself, maybe make a promise.

I promise to share my toys, ~~snacks~~ and be with a REAL freind.

Lesson 23: Listen Carefully

Understanding: Listening carefully means paying attention when others are speaking.

Real Life Application: When someone is talking to you, look at them and don't interrupt.

Story: The Tale of Sammy the Squirrel's Adventure

In the Whispering Woods, Sammy the squirrel set out on a grand adventure. His friends gave him important advice before he left. They told him to listen carefully to the rustling leaves, the bubbling brooks, and the wise old owls.

As Sammy journeyed through the Whispering Woods, he encountered many challenges. The rustling leaves whispered secrets that led him to hidden treasures, and the bubbling brooks shared stories of the forest's history. Sammy listened closely and learned about the lives of the creatures around him, forging new friendships.

One day, he met the wise old owl, Olivia, who shared the forest's deepest mysteries. Thanks to Sammy's attentive ears, he returned home with tales of his thrilling adventure and a deeper understanding of the Whispering Woods.

Consequence of Not Using: If you don't listen, you might miss important information or upset others.

Questions for Children:

1. Why is it important to listen when others are talking?

2. How does it feel when someone doesn't listen to you?

Perhaps you could write something here about this lesson' maybe your own experiences or how you could use it yourself, maybe make a promise.

Lesson 24: Be Grateful

Understanding: Gratitude means being thankful for the things you have.

Real Life Application: Say "thank you" when someone is kind to you, and appreciate your family and friends.

Story: The Tale of Ellie's Grateful Garden

In the village of Thanksburg, Ellie had a magical garden. It blossomed with the most vibrant flowers and delicious fruits. Every morning, she thanked the sun, the rain, and the soil for their gifts.

One day, a young traveler visited the village. Ellie shared her bountiful harvest with the traveler, and they enjoyed a feast together. The traveler, impressed by Ellie's kindness and gratitude, gifted her a rare seed. When planted, it grew into a tree that bore enchanted fruits, spreading happiness and thankfulness throughout the land.

Consequence of Not Using: If you're not grateful, people may not want to help or give to you.

Questions for Children:

1. What are you thankful for in your life?

2. How does saying "thank you" make you feel?

Perhaps you could write something here about this lesson' maybe your own experiences or how you could use it yourself, maybe make a promise.

Lesson 25: Responsibility Matters

Understanding: Responsibility means taking care of your tasks and doing your part.

Real Life Application: Complete your homework, chores, and take care of your pets.

Story: The Adventures of Ruby the Responsible Rabbit

In the peaceful village of Dutiful Dale, Ruby the Rabbit was known for her sense of responsibility. One day, a storm threatened the village. While some animals were nervous, Ruby sprang into action. She helped her neighbors secure their homes, collect food, and find shelter.

As the storm raged on, the animals of Dutiful Dale realized they had to work together. Ruby took charge, organizing teams to mend the damaged houses and provide food for those in need. Her actions united the village, and they weathered the storm with courage and unity.

Consequence of Not Using: If you're not responsible, important tasks may be left undone, causing problems for you and others.

Questions for Children:

1. What are some tasks you are responsible for at home or school?

2. How does it feel when someone is not responsible?

Perhaps you could write something here about this lesson' maybe your own experiences or how you could use it yourself, maybe make a promise.

Lesson 26: Empathy and Understanding

Understanding: Empathy means understanding how others feel and showing kindness towards them.

Real Life Application: Be a good listener, help a friend who's sad, and be there for others when they need support.

Story: The Tale of Emma the Empathetic Elephant

In the heart of the Enchanted Savannah, Emma the Elephant possessed a remarkable gift — empathy. She could sense the feelings of other animals in the Savannah, and she used her gift to offer comfort and support to those in need.

One day, Emma noticed a lonely lion named Leo, who had lost his way. She approached him with gentle words and a listening ear. Leo shared his worries and fears with Emma, who empathized with his feelings and helped him find his way back to his family.

As Emma's reputation for empathy spread, the animals of the Savannah started coming to her with their concerns. She organized group activities and shared stories that encouraged understanding and kindness. The Savannah became a place where every animal felt heard and valued.

Consequence of Not Using: If you lack empathy, you may not be able to support others effectively, and they may feel isolated.

Questions for Children:

1. How can you show empathy towards a friend who is sad or upset?

2. Why is it important to understand how others feel?

Perhaps you could write something here about this lesson' maybe your own experiences or how you could use it yourself, maybe make a promise.

Lesson 27: Perseverance Pays Off

Understanding: Perseverance means not giving up, even when things are difficult.

Real Life Application: Keep trying when you face challenges, practice to improve your skills, and work hard to achieve your goals.

Story: The Quest of Timmy the Tortoise

In the Land of Patience, lived Timmy the Tortoise, known for his remarkable perseverance. One sunny day, he heard about a great race that was taking place in the neighboring kingdom. Many animals were competing, including speedy hares and agile cheetahs.

Timmy decided to participate, even though he was the slowest of all. While others mocked him, he practiced every day, taking slow and steady steps. The race began, and Timmy lagged behind, but he never gave up.

As the other animals grew tired, Timmy, with his unwavering determination, overtook them one by one. In the end, he won the race through his patience and perseverance. The kingdom celebrated his triumph, and the other animals learned the value of persistence.

Consequence of Not Using: If you give up easily, you may miss out on opportunities and the chance to improve.

Questions for Children:

1. Can you think of a time when you had to work hard and persevere to achieve something?

2. Why is it important to never give up?

Perhaps you could write something here about this lesson' maybe your own experiences or how you could use it yourself, maybe make a promise.

Lesson 28: Respect for Nature

Understanding: Respect for nature means caring for the environment and the creatures that share the planet with us.

Real Life Application: Pick up litter, conserve water and energy, and treat animals with kindness.

Story: The Quest of Maya the Nature Guardian

In the mystical Forest of Harmony, Maya, a young guardian, was chosen by the ancient spirits to protect the forest and its creatures. She felt a deep connection with the animals and the trees and understood the importance of respecting nature.

One day, she discovered that the magical river, the life force of the forest, was polluted by careless travelers. Maya embarked on a journey to educate people about the importance of respecting the environment. She organized cleanup days and planted new trees. Her dedication to the forest inspired the travelers to change their ways.

The once-polluted river became crystal clear, and the animals of the forest thrived. Maya's respect for nature had a profound impact, and her forest remained a haven for generations to come.

Consequence of Not Using: If we don't respect nature, we harm our planet, leading to pollution, deforestation, and harm to wildlife.

Questions for Children:

1. What are some ways you can show respect for nature and the environment?

2. Why is it important to protect the environment?

Perhaps you could write something here about this lesson' maybe your own experiences or how you could use it yourself, maybe make a promise.

Lesson 29: Teamwork Triumphs

Understanding: Teamwork means working together with others to achieve a common goal.

Real Life Application: Cooperate with your classmates on group projects, play team sports, and help your family with chores.

Story: The Quest of the Diverse Crew

In the Kingdom of Unity, there was a legendary spaceship known as "Harmony Star." It could only be piloted by a diverse crew of animals with unique talents. A rabbit named Roger was an expert navigator, a squirrel named Sandy had quick reflexes, and a parrot named Polly was a skilled communicator.

One day, a meteor shower threatened their kingdom, and they were called into action. With teamwork and coordination, they guided the spaceship through the meteor shower, ensuring the safety of the kingdom. Each crew member's skills were essential, and they knew that by working together, they could achieve great things.

Their adventure inspired other animals to embrace teamwork and appreciate the power of diversity.

Consequence of Not Using: Without teamwork, it's challenging to accomplish larger goals and solve complex problems.

Questions for Children:

1. Can you think of a time when you worked as part of a team? How did it feel?

2. Why is teamwork important in our daily lives?

Perhaps you could write something here about this lesson' maybe your own experiences or how you could use it yourself, maybe make a promise.

Lesson 30: Respect for Others

Understanding: Respect for others means treating people with kindness and consideration, regardless of their differences.

Real Life Application: Be polite to everyone, listen to their opinions, and avoid making fun of others.

Story: The Tale of Amelia and the Bridge of Understanding*

In the village of Harmony Hills, there was a magical bridge known as the Bridge of Understanding. Amelia, a young deer, discovered it while exploring the hills. The bridge connected different parts of the village and brought together animals of various backgrounds.

Amelia noticed that the animals on the bridge always greeted each other with respect and kindness, regardless of their differences. She learned that respect for others made the village a harmonious place where everyone felt valued.

Amelia decided to organize a festival on the bridge, celebrating the diversity of the village. There were songs, dances, and delicious foods from every culture. The festival united the village, and the Bridge of Understanding became a symbol of respect and acceptance.

Consequence of Not Using: If you don't respect others, you may hurt their feelings and create conflicts.

Questions for Children:

1. How can you show respect for people who are different from you?

2. Why is it important to treat everyone with kindness and consideration?

Perhaps you could write something here about this lesson' maybe your own experiences or how you could use it yourself, maybe make a promise.

Lesson 31: The Gift of Kindness

Understanding: Kindness means being friendly, helpful, and considerate of others.

Real Life Application: Be kind to your friends, family, and even strangers you meet.

*Story: The Tale of Oliver and the Magic Stone**

In the peaceful meadow of Harmony Valley, a young rabbit named Oliver found a magical stone. This stone had the power to spread kindness. He decided to use it to make the world a better place.

Oliver performed small acts of kindness every day. He helped the birds build nests, shared food with the squirrels, and planted flowers to brighten the meadow. His acts of kindness inspired the other animals, and soon, the entire valley was filled with warmth and goodwill.

As a result, the meadow thrived, and the animals formed close bonds, creating a haven of kindness in Harmony Valley.

Consequence of Not Using: If you're unkind, you may hurt others' feelings and create a negative atmosphere.

Questions for Children:

1. Can you think of a time when someone was kind to you?

2. Why is it important to be kind to others?

Perhaps you could write something here about this lesson' maybe your own experiences or how you could use it yourself, maybe make a promise.

Lesson 32: Honesty and Trust

Understanding: Honesty builds trust, and trust is essential in any relationship.

Real Life Application: Be truthful in your words and actions, and you'll earn the trust of others.

*Story: The Quest of Leo the Loyal**

In the village of Truthville, Leo the Lynx was known for his unwavering honesty. One day, the village faced a crisis when a valuable gem, the Heartstone, went missing. Leo decided to solve the mystery and prove his loyalty to his village.

As he investigated, he found the Heartstone hidden in the woods. Instead of keeping it a secret, he returned it to the village. His honesty and loyalty earned the trust of his fellow villagers, and they celebrated the return of the Heartstone together.

Consequence of Not Using: If you're not honest, you may lose the trust of those you care about.

Questions for Children:

1. How does it feel when someone trusts you?
2. Why is honesty important in building trust?

Perhaps you could write something here about this lesson' maybe your own experiences or how you could use it yourself, maybe make a promise.

Lesson 33: The Magic of Sharing Knowledge

Understanding: Sharing knowledge means teaching others what you know to help them learn and grow.

Real Life Application: Help your classmates with their studies and share your skills to make the world a better place.

Story: The Tale of Luna and the Library of Enlightenment

Luna, the wise owl, discovered the Library of Enlightenment hidden in the Enchanted Forest. The library was filled with magical books that held knowledge beyond imagination. Luna realized the importance of sharing this knowledge with the world.

She opened the library to all creatures of the forest and spent her days teaching them what she had learned. As knowledge spread, the forest blossomed with new ideas, inventions, and art.

The creatures of the forest realized that the magic of sharing knowledge made their world a place of wisdom, innovation, and endless wonder.

Consequence of Not Using: If you don't share knowledge, you may limit the potential for growth and innovation in your community.

Questions for Children:

1. How does it feel to learn something new?

2. Why is it important to help others learn and grow?

Perhaps you could write something here about this lesson' maybe your own experiences or how you could use it yourself, maybe make a promise.

Lesson 34: The Power of Forgiveness

Understanding: Forgiveness means letting go of anger and resentment when someone hurts you.

Real Life Application: Forgive others when they apologize, and you'll free yourself from negativity.

*Story: The Tale of Ethan and the Stone of Forgiveness**

In the peaceful village of Serenity Glen, a special stone known as the Stone of Forgiveness was discovered by Ethan. This stone had the power to heal hearts and mend relationships.

Ethan used the Stone of Forgiveness to help those in the village who had conflicts. When people touched the stone, they were filled with compassion and the willingness to forgive. The village became a place where grudges were replaced by understanding and harmony.

Ethan realized that forgiveness was the key to inner peace, and he shared the Stone of Forgiveness with the world.

Consequence of Not Using: If you don't forgive, you might carry anger and hurt with you, affecting your happiness.

Questions for Children:

1. How does it feel to forgive someone who has hurt you?

2. Why is forgiveness important in maintaining healthy relationships?

Perhaps you could write something here about this lesson' maybe your own experiences or how you could use it yourself, maybe make a promise.

Lesson 35: The Magic of Curiosity

Understanding: Curiosity means being interested in learning and discovering new things.

Real Life Application: Ask questions, explore, and feed your curiosity to learn about the world.

*Story: The Quest of Alice and the Enchanted Telescope**

Alice, a young rabbit, found an Enchanted Telescope in her grandmother's attic. When she looked through it, she could see faraway lands and distant galaxies. Her curiosity led her on a journey to explore the mysteries of the universe.

She traveled through the stars, encountered friendly aliens, and learned about the wonders of the cosmos. Her journey was filled with curiosity and excitement, and she returned to her village with a heart full of stories to share.

Consequence of Not Using: If you're not curious, you might miss out on the joy of discovering new things.

Questions for Children:

1. What's something you're curious about right now?

2. How does curiosity help us learn and grow?

Perhaps you could write something here about this lesson' maybe your own experiences or how you could use it yourself, maybe make a promise.

Lesson 36: The Beauty of Friendship Bonds

Understanding: Friendships are built on trust, kindness, and spending time together.

Real Life Application: Make friends by being friendly, and nurture those friendships through shared experiences.

Story: The Tale of Finn and the Friendship Tree

Finn, a young squirrel, discovered a magnificent Friendship Tree in the heart of the forest. The tree grew beautiful, glowing fruit that had the power to strengthen bonds between friends. Finn decided to share the fruit with his friends, and together they created the most remarkable friendships.

As they spent time together, they played games, shared stories, and supported each other. Their bonds grew stronger with each passing day, and their friendships became the foundation of happiness and joy in the forest.

Consequence of Not Using: If you don't make an effort to be friendly and build friendships, you might miss out on wonderful connections.

Questions for Children:

1. How do you make a new friend?

2. Why is it important to spend time with your friends?

Perhaps you could write something here about this lesson' maybe your own experiences or how you could use it yourself, maybe make a promise.

Lesson 37: The Gift of Positivity

Understanding: Positivity means having a cheerful and hopeful attitude even in challenging times.

Real Life Application: Stay positive, find the bright side of things, and spread joy to those around you.

*Story: The Tale of Oscar and the Cloud of Cheer**

Oscar, a young raccoon, discovered a Cloud of Cheer that floated over his village. This magical cloud had the power to make everyone feel happy and positive. Oscar realized the cloud was drawn to positive energy, so he started spreading cheer throughout the village.

He organized games, told funny jokes, and celebrated small victories. The more positivity he shared, the larger the Cloud of Cheer grew. Eventually, the entire village was enveloped in an atmosphere of happiness and hope.

Oscar learned that positivity was a gift that could brighten even the darkest days.

Consequence of Not Using: If you're not positive, you might miss out on opportunities to make yourself and others happy.

Questions for Children:

1. How do you stay positive when things don't go your way?

2. Why is it important to spread cheer to others?

Perhaps you could write something here about this lesson' maybe your own experiences or how you could use it yourself, maybe make a promise.

Lesson 38: The Strength of Empathy

Understanding: Empathy means understanding and caring about how others feel.

Real Life Application: Be there for friends and family when they're sad, and show compassion to those who are going through difficult times.

*Story: The Tale of Emma and the Bridge of Compassion**

In the village of Empathy Cove, a magical bridge known as the Bridge of Compassion connected the hearts of the villagers. Emma, a young deer, discovered the bridge one day. It allowed her to feel the emotions of others.

Emma used her gift to comfort and support those who were hurting. When someone was sad, she crossed the bridge to be with them, offering a listening ear and a kind word. The village became a place where everyone shared their joys and sorrows, creating a strong sense of community.

Emma learned that empathy was the key to understanding and caring for others.

Consequence of Not Using: If you're not empathetic, you might find it challenging to comfort and support those in need.

Questions for Children:

1. How do you show empathy to a friend who is going through a tough time?

2. Why is it important to understand how others feel?

Perhaps you could write something here about this lesson' maybe your own experiences or how you could use it yourself, maybe make a promise.

Lesson 39: The Magic of Imagination

Understanding: Imagination means creating stories, ideas, and pictures in your mind.

Real Life Application: Use your imagination to solve problems, create art, and have fun adventures.

Story: The Quest of Lily and the Enchanted Paintbrush*

In the town of Wonderwood, Lily was a young artist with a magical paintbrush. Anything she painted came to life. Lily used her imagination to create a world filled with talking animals, flying ships, and floating castles.

Her adventures were filled with excitement as she explored the imaginative world she had painted. She realized that the power of imagination was a key to unlocking endless possibilities.

Consequence of Not Using: Without imagination, life may seem less exciting and creative.

Questions for Children:

1. How can you use your imagination to make your day more fun?

2. Why is imagination important in problem-solving?

Perhaps you could write something here about this lesson' maybe your own experiences or how you could use it yourself, maybe make a promise.

Lesson 40: The Gift of Respect for Elders

Understanding: Respect for elders means showing consideration and appreciation for those who are older and wiser.

Real Life Application: Listen to their stories, ask for their advice, and show gratitude for their wisdom.

Story: The Tale of Sophia and the Grand Oak Tree

In the heart of the forest, Sophia, a young rabbit, found the Grand Oak Tree, a wise and ancient tree that had witnessed the passage of time. She visited the tree daily and listened to its stories, which were as old as the forest itself.

As Sophia showed respect and appreciation for the Grand Oak Tree, she also learned valuable lessons about the forest's history and secrets. She shared the knowledge she gained with her friends, and the forest became a place where everyone respected their elders and learned from their wisdom.

Sophia understood that respect for elders was a way of preserving knowledge and tradition.

Consequence of Not Using: If you don't respect your elders, you might miss out on their valuable wisdom and experiences.

Questions for Children:

1. What can you learn from your grandparents or other elders in your life?

2. Why is it important to show respect for older people?

Perhaps you could write something here about this lesson' maybe your own experiences or how you could use it yourself, maybe make a promise.

Lesson 41: The Art of Patience

Understanding: Patience means waiting calmly without getting upset.

Real Life Application: Practice patience when waiting your turn or facing delays, and you'll avoid unnecessary frustration.

Story: The Quest of Oliver and the Slow Stream*

In the tranquil woods of Stillbrook, Oliver, a young otter, encountered a slow-flowing stream. He was determined to cross to the other side, but it required great patience.

Oliver tried to rush across but fell into the stream. Wet and discouraged, he realized that patience was the key. He watched the stream and noticed that it had its own rhythm. By waiting for the right moment, he was able to cross without a problem.

Oliver's experience taught him the value of patience, and he shared this lesson with his friends, who learned to embrace patience in their lives.

Consequence of Not Using: If you lack patience, you might become frustrated easily and make hasty decisions.

Questions for Children:

1. Can you think of a time when you had to be patient?
2. Why is patience important in daily life?

> Perhaps you could write something here about this lesson' maybe your own experiences or how you could use it yourself, maybe make a promise.

Lesson 42: The Gift of Generosity

Understanding: Generosity means sharing what you have with others.

Real Life Application: Give to those in need, and you'll experience the joy of helping others.

Story: The Tale of Mia and the Sharing Festival

Mia, a kind-hearted mouse, lived in a village where the Sharing Festival was celebrated. During this event, everyone shared food, clothes, and toys with those who had less.

Mia participated with enthusiasm, sharing her most treasured belongings. The festival created an atmosphere of love and togetherness, and the village became a place where generosity was a way of life.

Mia learned that generosity was a gift that could make the world a better place.

Consequence of Not Using: If you're not generous, you may miss out on the joy of helping others and building stronger connections.

Questions for Children:

1. How does it feel to share with someone who needs it?

2. Why is generosity important in our world?

> Perhaps you could write something here about this lesson' maybe your own experiences or how you could use it yourself, maybe make a promise.

Lesson 43: The Magic of Perseverance

Understanding: Perseverance means continuing to work hard even when things get tough.

Real Life Application: Keep trying, and you'll achieve your goals and overcome challenges.

*Story: The Quest of Leo and the Steep Mountain**

Leo the lion lived at the base of a steep mountain. He had a dream of reaching the summit, but the path was filled with obstacles. Leo started climbing and faced many challenges, but he never gave up.

Through determination and hard work, he reached the summit and discovered breathtaking views. His journey taught him that perseverance was the key to achieving his dreams. He returned to the village as a symbol of determination and inspired others to overcome their challenges.

Consequence of Not Using: If you don't persevere, you may give up on your dreams and never discover your full potential.

Questions for Children:

1. Can you think of a time when you had to work hard to achieve something?

2. Why is perseverance important in life?

Perhaps you could write something here about this lesson' maybe your own experiences or how you could use it yourself, maybe make a promise.

Lesson 44: The Gift of Listening

Understanding: Listening means paying attention when others are speaking.

Real Life Application: Be a good listener, and you'll build better relationships and understand others.

*Story: The Tale of Sammy the Squirrel's Adventure**

Sammy, a curious squirrel, embarked on an adventure to explore his forest home. Along the way, he encountered many creatures, each with their own stories to tell.

Sammy listened intently to their tales, showing genuine interest. His kind ears became a safe space for others to share their thoughts and feelings. Sammy's listening created strong bonds and made the forest a place of understanding and connection.

Sammy learned that being a good listener was a gift that could bring people closer together.

Consequence of Not Using: If you don't listen, you might miss important information and upset others.

Questions for Children:

1. Why is it important to listen when others are talking?
2. How does it feel when someone doesn't listen to you?

Perhaps you could write something here about this lesson' maybe your own experiences or how you could use it yourself, maybe make a promise.

Lesson 45: The Joy of Learning

Understanding: The joy of learning means finding happiness in discovering new things and gaining knowledge.

Real Life Application: Be curious, ask questions, read books, and explore new subjects.

Story: The Quest of Oliver and the Book of Wonders

In the Library of Enchantment, Oliver, a young owl, found an ancient Book of Wonders. The book contained stories of faraway lands, magical creatures, and hidden secrets. Oliver was fascinated and decided to embark on a quest to uncover these wonders.

As he read and learned, he shared the stories with his friends, and they all became curious about the world around them. Together, they discovered that the joy of learning was a magical journey in itself, full of surprises and endless possibilities.

Consequence of Not Using: If you don't embrace the joy of learning, you may miss out on the excitement of discovering new things.

Questions for Children:

1. What do you enjoy learning about the most?

2. Why is learning important in life?

Perhaps you could write something here about this lesson' maybe your own experiences or how you could use it yourself, maybe make a promise.

Lesson 46: Gratitude for Family

Understanding: Gratitude for family means being thankful for the love and support of your family members.

Real Life Application: Say "thank you" to your family, spend quality time together, and express your love for them.

Story: The Tale of Mia's Magical Thank-You Letters*

Mia was a young mouse who discovered the magic of thank-you letters. She wrote heartfelt notes to her family, thanking them for their love and support. Her letters brought smiles and warmth to her family's hearts.

In return, Mia's family organized a special day to express their gratitude. They spent the day together, sharing stories, playing games, and enjoying a picnic. Their love and appreciation for one another made their family bonds even stronger.

Consequence of Not Using: If you're not grateful for your family, you might take their love and support for granted, leading to strained relationships.

Questions for Children:

1. What do you love the most about your family?
2. How does it feel when someone in your family says "thank you"?

> Perhaps you could write something here about this lesson' maybe your own experiences or how you could use it yourself, maybe make a promise.
>
> I promise to be grateful for my family and relitives and say "Thank you for being my (e.g Sister or cousin/Uncle/parents/Anti?!
>
> † * * ♡ † *

Lesson 47: The Adventure of Honesty

Understanding: Honesty means telling the truth even when it's difficult.

Real Life Application: Always be truthful, even if you've made a mistake.

Story: The Quest of Prince Leo and the Magic Mirror*

In the kingdom of Verityville, Prince Leo discovered a magical mirror that only revealed the truth. He asked the mirror if he was the best archer in the land, but it showed his true skills. Leo knew he needed to practice harder, so he committed himself to becoming the best archer through honesty and dedication.

As Leo's archery skills improved, he met other young knights who admired his hard work and dedication. They started the "Honest Knights" club, where they not only honed their skills but also helped others in the kingdom. They organized archery competitions and awarded prizes to those who displayed honesty and integrity.

Their club flourished, and Prince Leo became known not only for his archery but also for his unwavering honesty. He grew up to be a beloved and respected ruler who valued truth and fairness above all.

Consequence of Not Using: If you're not honest, people may not trust you.

Questions for Children:

1. Can you think of a time when telling the truth was hard but important?

2. How do you feel when someone lies to you?

> Perhaps you could write something here about this lesson' maybe your own experiences or how you could use it yourself, maybe make a promise.

Lesson 48: Sharing Makes Friends

Understanding: Sharing means giving part of what you have to someone else.

Real Life Application: Share your toys, snacks, or time with a friend.

Story: The Tale of Luna and the Magic Seeds

In the secret Garden of Serendipity, Luna the fox discovered magical seeds that grew into beautiful flowers. She decided to share these seeds with her animal friends. Luna's act of generosity not only brought her friends together but also attracted butterflies, bees, and birds who helped her garden bloom into the most splendid place in the forest. It became a haven for all creatures to enjoy together.

The creatures of the garden decided to organize a grand celebration. They created fun games like hide-and-seek among the flowers, flying races with the butterflies, and a special feast with fruits from the garden. New friendships bloomed, and Luna's garden became a place of joy and togetherness for all.

Consequence of Not Using: If you don't share, you might not have as many friends to play with.

Questions for Children:

1. How does sharing make you feel?

2. Why is it important to share with others?

Perhaps you could write something here about this lesson' maybe your own experiences or how you could use it yourself, maybe make a promise.

Lesson 49: Listen Carefully

Understanding: Listening carefully means paying attention when others are speaking.

Real Life Application: When someone is talking to you, look at them and don't interrupt.

Story: The Tale of Sammy the Squirrel's Adventure

In the Whispering Woods, Sammy the squirrel set out on a grand adventure. His friends gave him important advice before he left. They told him to listen carefully to the rustling leaves, the bubbling brooks, and the wise old owls.

As Sammy journeyed through the Whispering Woods, he encountered many challenges. The rustling leaves whispered secrets that led him to hidden treasures, and the bubbling brooks shared stories of the forest's history. Sammy listened closely and learned about the lives of the creatures around him, forging new friendships.

One day, he met the wise old owl, Olivia, who shared the forest's deepest mysteries. Thanks to Sammy's attentive ears, he returned home with tales of his thrilling adventure and a deeper understanding of the Whispering Woods.

Consequence of Not Using: If you don't listen, you might miss important information or upset others.

Questions for Children:

1. Why is it important to listen when others are talking?

2. How does it feel when someone doesn't listen to you?

> Perhaps you could write something here about this lesson' maybe your own experiences or how you could use it yourself, maybe make a promise.

Lesson 50: Be Grateful

Understanding: Gratitude means being thankful for the things you have.

Real Life Application: Say "thank you" when someone is kind to you, and appreciate your family and friends.

Story: The Tale of Ellie's Grateful Garden*

In the village of Thanksburg, Ellie had a magical garden. It blossomed with the most vibrant flowers and delicious fruits. Every morning, she thanked the sun, the rain, and the soil for their gifts.

One day, a young traveler visited the village. Ellie shared her bountiful harvest with the traveler, and they enjoyed a feast together. The traveler, impressed by Ellie's kindness and gratitude, gifted her a rare seed. When planted, it grew into a tree that bore enchanted fruits, spreading happiness and thankfulness throughout the land.

Consequence of Not Using: If you're not grateful, people may not want to help or give to you.

Questions for Children:

1. What are you thankful for in your life?

2. How does saying "thank you" make you feel?

Perhaps you could write something here about this Life Lesson' maybe your own experiences or how you could use it yourself, maybe make a promise.